EVERY ACTION COUNTS!

Helping Others

By Belinda Gallagher

Ruby Tuesday Books

Published in 2024 by Ruby Tuesday Books Ltd.

Copyright © 2024 Ruby Tuesday Books Ltd.

All rights reserved. No part of this publication may be reproduced in whole or in part, stored in any retrieval system, or transmitted in any form or by any means, electronic, mechanical, photocopying, recording, or otherwise, without written permission from the publisher.

Editors: Ruth Owen & Mark J. Sachner
Production: John Lingham

Photo credits:
Alamy: 3TL (Frances Roberts), 18B (Tony Watson), 26C (Fredrick Kippe), 28BR (Jeffrey Isaac Greenberg 3+); Shutterstock: Cover TL (Irina Wilhauk), cover CL (Dmitry Demidovich), cover BL (Ground Picture), cover TR (VH-studio), cover CR (Kraken Images), cover BR (Ryan DeBerardinis), 4T (DGL Images), 4C (Dragon Images), 4B (SeventyFour), 5T (Anna Stills), 5BR (Anastasiya Aleksandrenko), 6TR (Khosro), 6C (Monkey Business Images & etorres), 6B (Monkey Business Images), 7T (fizkes), 7CL (fizkes), 7CR (ESB Professional), 7B (fizkes), 8T (Wave Break Media), 8CL (Robert Kneschke), 8CR (Juan Brian Diaz Hernandez), 8B (Robyn Mackenzie), 9T (Studio_G & Xeniya Bennu), 10T (PeopleImages.com – Yuri A), 10C (Monkey Business Images), 10B (panyajampatong), 11TL (Tatyana Vyc), 11TR (Irina Wilhauk), 12T (Robert Kneschke), 12CL (Lopolo), 12CR (Bear Fotos), 12B (Veja), 13T (Kraken Images), 13CL (Africa Studio), 13BR (PeopleImages.com – Yuri A), 14T (Iryna Inshyna), 14C (MEDIAIMAG), 14BL (Master1305), 14BR (Sergey Novikov), 15T (Vagengeim), 15C (New Africa), 15BL (Ground Picture), 16T (MPH Photos), 16CR (Juice Dash), 16CL (Monkey Business Images), 16B (Richard A. McGuirk), 17T (Anastasia Panait), 17B (Only Zoia), 18 (Wave Break Media, Jacob Lund, Treerat Wongvorapat, Tyler Olson, Drazen Zigic, SeventyFour, VAKS Stock Agency, Kzenon, ESB Professional), 19T (ChameleonsEye), 19C (SeventyFour), 19B (13Smile), 20T (Ground Picture), 20CL (Wave Break Media), 20CR (PeopleImages.com – Yuri A), 20B (Inside Creative House), 21L (Monkey Business Images), 22T (PeopleImages.com – Yuri A), 22CR (Halfpoint), 22CL (Bear Fotos), 22B (PeopleImages.com – Yuri A), 23TR (EvgeniiAnd), 23BL (Lester Balajadia), 23BR (Mikhail Gnatkovskiy), 24T (Darrin Heny), 24C (Dmytro Zinkevych), 24B (Dmytro Zinkevych), 25T (Bear Fotos), 25CR (Veja), 26T (SeventyFour), 26BL (Wave Break Media), 26BR (Luis Louro), 27TL (somrak jendee), 27TR (Pressmaster), 27BR (Joanne Dale), 28T (VaLiza), 28C (Dmytro Zinkevych), 28BL (Monkey Business Images), 29B (Chay_Tee), 30TL (Ground Picture), 30BL (Monkey Business Images), 30R (Africa Studio), 31TL (In Green), 31BL (Paulaphoto), 31TR (Ground Picture), 31BR (Kraken Images).

ISBN 978-1-78856-445-8

Printed in Poland by L&C Printing Group

www.rubytuesdaybooks.com

Note from the Publisher

Neither the publisher nor the author can accept legal responsibility or liability for any loss, harm or injury that may come about from following the instructions in this book. All activities should be carried out with adult guidance and supervision. Some activities involve being out of doors in public spaces. Children should be accompanied at all times. It is the parent's or carer's responsibility to ensure their child is safe.

CONTENTS

How Can You Help Others?..4

You're Important, Too!..6

Just Smile 8

Helping Out at Home..10

Looking Out for Friends..12

Share Your Skills...14

Let's Be Good Neighbours...16

People Who Help Us...18

Helping Others at School..20

Little Actions in Your Community...22

Offering Your Time...24

Causes You Care About...26

Every Action Counts!..28

Glossary...30

Index..32

Staying Safe!

All the activities in this book are fun and easy to do. Be sure to ask an adult to help you with each one at every stage. Never go anywhere without your trusted adult. Wear old clothes for the make-and-do activities. Some activities need scissors. Always ask for help when using sharp things. When outside, make sure you are wearing clothes that suit the weather. Have fun!

How Can You Help Others?

Helping other people is about showing **kindness**. When you are kind and friendly, it makes other people feel happy.

Helping with everyday tasks is a simple way to show you care.

Did you know?
Helping others is good for you! It makes you feel happy, and this helps keep you healthy.

Can you help with shopping in the supermarket and putting groceries away?

Top Tip
Ask a friend or family member how they are today – especially if they seem sad or **worried**. This thoughtful question could brighten their day.

Listen to a friend as they talk. They may be telling you about their day or an activity. They will be pleased you took the time to listen to them.

Did you know?

If you listen to your friends, they will listen to you, too. This is a great way to help each other.

Make Happy Jars

Make a jar of happy thoughts and memories that will keep you and your family smiling.

You will need:
- Containers with lids (such as empty jars)
- Small pieces of paper
- Pens or pencils

1. Every day, write down one happy moment you've had. It can be something simple like a sunny walk to school or a kind comment from a teacher. Be sure to add a date.

   02/02/2024
   Miss Johnson said I'm a really good team player!

2. Encourage your family members to make their own happy jars.

3. Include little reminders of happy days spent outdoors, such as seashells or pine cones, in your jars.

4. Whenever you or someone else feels sad, take one happy memory from your jar.

How do you feel when you read your note?

5

You're Important, Too!

Sometimes we forget to take care of ourselves because the world is so busy. **Self-care** is about taking little actions to keep you happy and healthy.

EAT HEALTHY FOOD

This will give your body all the goodness it needs. Make healthy meals and snacks with other people in your home.

Did you know?

Feeling grateful for little things in your day makes you feel good. It could be a simple hug or some friendly words.

GET OUTSIDE

Go outside and enjoy nature in parks, woodlands and on beaches. Sunshine and fresh air are good for your body, and being in nature makes you feel happy.

MOVE YOUR BODY

Exercise is good for every part of you, from your heart to your brain. Dance in the kitchen and living room, skip around the garden – every action counts!

ENJOY SLEEPING

Sleep helps you recover from your busy day. It also helps your body grow and repair itself. How do you feel after a good night's sleep?

Being Mindful

Next time you are outside in nature, try this simple activity. You could be at the park on a picnic or in your garden.

You will need:
- All you need is yourself and a few spare minutes.

1. Relax in a comfortable position. Focus on where you are. Try not to think of anything else.

2. Name three things that you can see.

3. Name three things that you can hear. Perhaps birds are singing.

4. Name something that you can feel. This might be the grass or simply the ground under your feet.

5. Name something that you can smell, such as nice fresh air.

Well done! You have practised being present and mindful. How do you feel?

Top Tip

Everyone feels sad sometimes. This is okay. Don't keep worries to yourself. Try talking to someone you know and trust, and tell them how you feel.

Just Smile

Smiling is an easy way to help others. People smile to say hello, be friendly and make others feel welcome. A simple smile makes people feel cared about.

SHARE A SNACK!

Sharing is a kind action. Offer to share a snack with friends. Do they smile and say thank you?

MAKE SOMEONE LAUGH TODAY

Make a funny face or tell a silly joke. Laughing is even better than smiling!

MAKE A SMILEY SNACK

Use vegetables and salad to make a fun – and healthy – snack for a loved one.

Did you know?

When we smile, our brains release special chemicals that lift our mood and make us feel relaxed.

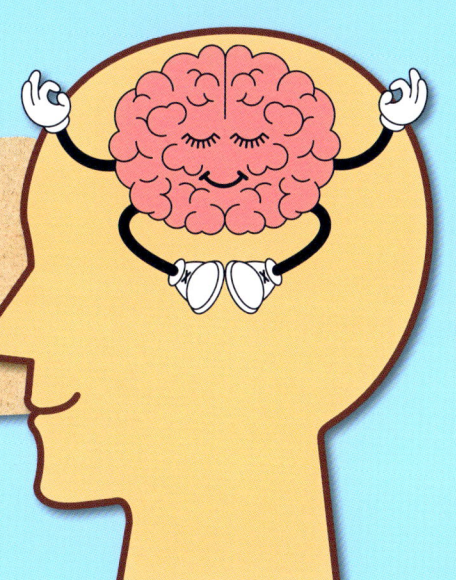

Top Tip

When you smile at someone, they smile back. Use your smile to cheer someone up or tell them how proud you are of them.

Smile Experiment

Try this fun experiment and see how many smiles you can raise today.

You will need:
- Some paper
- A pen or pencil

1 Who did you smile at?	2 Where was this?	3 When was this?	4 Did they smile back?

1. Copy this chart onto the paper and add as many rows as you need.

2. Write the names of people you smiled at in the first column. If you don't know their name, describe who they were, such as the postman.

3. Add where you were when the smile happened, and the time of day in column 3.

4. Finally, write what happened when you smiled at each person in column 4.

What did you discover from your smile experiment?

Helping Out at Home

Sharing jobs and chores at home is helpful for everyone. It isn't fair to leave all the chores to other people.

By working as a team, doing chores is more fun and there is less work for everyone.

Laying the table or helping prepare a meal are great ways to help out.

Did you know?

Helping your family makes you feel closer to them. And when everyone plays a small part, jobs soon get done.

Perhaps a brother or sister needs help with homework or an art project. Maybe a young family member can't tie their shoelaces or button their coat.

Our pets need help, too. Share their care by taking your turn to feed, walk or groom them.

Make your bed and keep your room tidy. Make chores fun by singing your favourite song or dancing as you tidy up.

Choose a Chore Stick

Make these chore sticks to help get chores done quickly. Then you'll have more time for fun.

You will need:
- 1 jar for the chore sticks
- 1 jar per person helping with chores
- 1 jar for completed chore sticks
- Paper
- Scissors
- Marker pens
- Sticky tape or glue
- About 30 lolly or craft sticks

1. Cut labels from the paper. Write your family's names on the labels and stick them to the jars.

2. Cut out and write two more labels. One should say CHORES and the other should say COMPLETE. Stick each label to a jar.

3. With your family, write a list of chores.

4. Write each chore on a stick and put the sticks in the CHORES jar.

5. Everyone now chooses chores and puts the sticks they've chosen in their jar. When a chore is finished, add the stick to the COMPLETE jar.

Looking Out for Friends

Friends are people you choose to spend time with. You may have lots of friends, or just a few. Good friends look out for each other.

If one of your friends feels sad, talk to them and listen to them. Try to understand how they are feeling by remembering a time when you felt sad.

Enjoy fun activities with friends. Sharing happy times is good for you and them.

Sometimes friends may not agree. This is okay. But try not to lose your temper. Shouting at a friend is not a good way to act.

It's important to say "I'm sorry" to a friend if you have upset them.

Say hi to a friend you haven't seen for a while. You can call or visit them. They will be happy you have been thinking of them.

Top Tip
Our friends are all different. Some may be shy or afraid to join in. Try to include them in the things you do to help them feel braver.

Make a Friendship Den

This cosy den is a happy space to spend time with your friends!

You will need:
- Chairs or a table
- Blankets, sheets and sleeping bags
- Clothes pegs and books
- Cushions
- Strings of lights
- Games and snacks

3. Use pegs to clip strings of lights outside and inside the den.

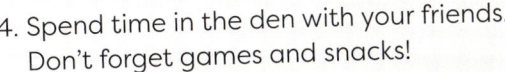

1. Choose an indoor space for your den. Throw blankets or sheets over the chairs or a table to create a covered tent-like den. Use pegs or piles of books to hold the coverings in place.

2. Add blankets or sleeping bags to the floor of your tent and lots of cushions.

4. Spend time in the den with your friends. Don't forget games and snacks!

Share Your Skills

What are you good at? Can you create cool art, play chess or bake delicious cookies? We are all good at different things. By showing others how to do something, you can help them learn new **skills**.

If you are good at reading or writing, practise with someone who may need help.

You might be good at riding a bike or roller-skating. Offer to show someone else how to do it.

Can you teach someone in your family how to use a touchscreen or a new app? They will be pleased to learn something so useful.

Remember! The person you are helping may need time to learn the skills you are sharing.

Top Tip
Ask a friend or family member to show YOU how to do something. It could be computer coding, dancing or playing a musical instrument. Keep practising your new skill – you will soon improve!

Did you know?
It's fun showing someone how to do something new. It could be helping a younger brother or sister learn how to tie their shoes, or helping your best friend learn to swim.

Plan Some Skill Shares

Be the teacher
Think about your friends and family. Is someone you know struggling to do something that you are good at? Offer to be their teacher. This is a very kind action.

Be the student
Think about your friends and family. Does someone you know have a skill you'd like to learn? Ask to be their student. Being asked to help will make them feel great!

Remember! All skills are important – no matter how simple.

Let's Be Good Neighbours

Our neighbours are the people who live close to us. You are someone's neighbour, too! Being a good neighbour means being friendly and helpful.

Did you know?
Good neighbours make a happy neighbourhood. Can you smile at a neighbour today? A wave or smile could make their day better.

You may have a new neighbour. Ask a trusted adult if you can try to make friends.

If you have new neighbours, be friendly and ask them to join in with your activities.

Offer to help older neighbours or neighbours with disabilities with everyday tasks or simple chores. This could be opening a gate, carrying their shopping or helping them in their garden.

STAY SAFE
Never visit neighbours alone. Always have a trusted adult with you.

Did you know?

Having good neighbours can make us feel safe and secure. When you're friendly to neighbours, they will know they can rely on you and your family to lend a hand if they need help.

Sharing homemade gifts is a thoughtful action.

Bake some cookies and deliver them to neighbours. Always ask an adult to go with you.

Make No-Grow Flowers

Try this activity to make a fun gift that will cheer up a neighbour who is sad, lonely or feeling unwell.

You will need:
- A pencil
- A ruler
- Coloured craft paper, including green
- Scissors
- A glue stick

1. Using a pencil and ruler, draw a kite shape on one piece of paper and cut it out.

2. Next draw a triangle that's the same size, shape and colour as the bottom of the kite shape. Cut it out.

3. On the green paper, draw three thin flower stems that are shorter than the triangle. Cut these out.

4. Now draw and cut out three flower shapes. Glue these to the stems. Cut out and glue a circle to the centre of each flower.

5. Place the three flowers on the kite shape. Then glue the triangle on top of the kite shape and flowers.

Your No-Grow Flowers are ready for delivery!

17

People Who Help Us

There are lots of different people who work hard to help us in our communities. Can YOU give a little back and make someone's day happier?

Teacher

Shop assistant

Doctor

Librarian

Bus driver

Parcel delivery person

Vet

Firefighter

Refuse collector

Dentist

Give your postman or postwoman a wave and a smile. They will appreciate it!

18

Make people's jobs a little easier. Always sort and recycle rubbish properly. Make sure your dustbin and recycling are outside on time.

Be polite and say "good morning" to someone. This little action says big things.

Help pack the groceries at the supermarket, and thank the shop assistant for serving you.

Make a thank-you note for your teacher, and ask your classmates to sign it. It will make your teacher proud and happy.

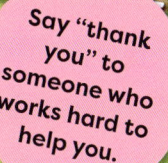

Say "thank you" to someone who works hard to help you.

How Are You?

Have you noticed how shop assistants are polite and friendly? This makes us feel cared for and valued.

Try asking this simple question next time you are served in a shop. "How are you today?"

What happens?

Did you know?

When you are kind, other people will want to be kind, too. This is how kindness spreads to make the world a happier place.

Helping Others at School

School is a place where you learn, join in with fun activities and make friends. There are lots of actions you can take to make school a happy place for everyone.

Welcome a new classmate! Be friendly and show them around to help them settle in.

If someone is on their own at lunchtime, ask them to sit with you.

Help others with a tricky task. Working in a group is fun, too.

Top Tip
If a school friend is feeling sad or you are worried about a classmate, tell a teacher that they might need help.

Start a Kindness Club

Ask your teacher if you can start a kindness club to spread kindness around your school!

You will need:
- Pens and paper
- A teacher
- A place to meet at school
- School friends

1. Write down your reasons for starting a kindness club. Talk them through with your teacher.

2. Decide how often you want your club to meet and where.

3. Ask your school friends if they would like to be members. Decide the date for your first meeting.

4. Hold your first meeting. All the members can think up activities the club would like to do. Starting small is best. There is a list of ideas on the right.

5. Choose an activity to complete before your next meeting, and start spreading kindness!

Make "Positive Thinking" posters and put them around your school.

Paint kindness rocks and leave them around your school or town (see page 23).

Bring in food in cans and packets and make up a box to **donate** to a food bank.

Organise a litter pick on the streets around your school.

Write stories and poems about kindness.

Bake cookies and bring them in to share with your classmates.

Make kindness badges or a "Kindest Student" award.

At your next meeting, talk about what you did. What did you learn from that activity? Repeat!

Little Actions in Your Community

A **community** is a group of people who live, work, learn and play in the same area, such as a town or city. A community may have homes, shops, schools and hospitals.

With your family, check out what there is to do near you. Your local community centre may run clubs and activities to bring neighbours and new friends together.

ART AND CRAFTS

DANCING, SINGING OR DRAMA

Did you know?
Being part of a community makes us feel safe and connects us to others.

Did you know?
Every person in a community is important. By taking time to join in, you can make a difference and help make your community stronger.

SPORTS

Find out if you can visit an animal rescue centre with your family. Ask the volunteers if there are ways that you can help.

Top Tip
Remember that volunteering is about doing simple actions. The small things you do to help others are important. Every little action helps!

Fill a Donation Box

You can donate useful items to an animal rescue centre or a **charity** that supports people who are in need. Collect items from your home and ask your friends to donate, too.

You will need:
- A sturdy box
- Items to donate

1. Decide where you would like to donate your box. For an animal rescue centre, you could collect blankets, towels, unwanted pet toys and pet food. For a charity that helps people in need, you could collect clothes, toys and long-lasting food in tins and packets.

3. When you have enough items to fill your box, arrange to deliver it with your family.

2. Fill your box over time. For example, you could buy a food item each week when your family does their food shopping.

25

Causes You Care About

Helping others doesn't cost a thing. But people can also come together to raise money for a charity or good cause. There are lots of fun ways to do this. Could you raise some money to help out?

Write a list of issues that are important to you. Here are some ideas to get you started:

- Finding new homes for unwanted pets
- Buying equipment for your school
- Protecting local wildlife
- Cleaning up the **environment**

ENTER A SPONSORED WALK OR RUN

People **sponsor** you to walk or run a certain distance. The money you raise goes to your chosen charity.

WASH CARS

Offer to wash your neighbours' cars for a small donation.

ARRANGE A CLASS OR SCHOOL COSTUME DAY

Each person taking part pays a small amount of money to wear a costume. The money goes towards a fund-raising project at your school.

MAKE A GIVING JAR

Recycle a glass jar and ask your family to add spare coins to it whenever they can. Donate the money to your chosen cause.

HOLD A GARAGE SALE

Sell unwanted books, games and clothes to raise money. Let your community know about your sale well in advance.

Organise a School Bake Sale

Ask your teacher for permission to hold a bake sale to raise money for a cause you care about. Here are some ideas and tips to help your sale go smoothly.

- With your teacher and your classmates who want to take part, choose a date for the sale. Decide who will bake which treats.

- On the day, decorate a classroom with homemade paper chains. Bring tablecloths from home to cover desks.

- Don't forget to bring in some coins so you can give your customers change.

Cookies   Brownies   Cupcakes

Let your sale begin, and raise lots of money!

- To keep things simple, decide on one price that you will charge per cake or cookie.

- Draw posters and make flyers to advertise your sale.

- Make a plan for the day of the sale so that everyone knows what to do and when.

- Bake everything the day before!

Every Action Counts!

Helping others begins with small actions. A smile, a wave and some kind words can make a big difference.

Top Tip
When you have finished this book, share it with friends. You can encourage them to be kind and caring, too. How awesome is that?

Always be kind.

Make time for friends and talk to them if they seem sad.

Care about neighbours.

Treat others in a friendly, thoughtful way.

Remember that everyone needs to help out with chores at home.

Care about your community and volunteer to help with local projects.

Be a good friend.

Kindness Calendar

Make a monthly calendar of kind actions you can take. Remember, your actions need only be small.

You will need:
- A large piece of cardstock paper
- A ruler
- Pencils

Copy this chart onto the paper. Write in actions for each day. We've made some suggestions, but you can think up your own ideas, too.

	MONDAY	TUESDAY	WEDNESDAY	THURSDAY	FRIDAY
Week 1	Make a happy jar for someone you care about.	:)	Pick up litter when you go for a walk.	:)	Ask a worker how they are today.
Week 2	Smile at the first person you see. Tell them to have a nice day.	Call a friend to say hi.	Donate old clothes to a local charity shop.	:)	Help someone at home with a chore.
Week 3	Share your favourite game with a friend.	Paint a kindness stone and leave it for a neighbour to find.	Help a classmate with an activity or task.	Share a snack with a classmate.	Ask a friend over for a play date.
Week 4	Offer to make a snack or a drink for someone at home.	:)	Make someone laugh.	:)	Sow some wildflower seeds in your garden – the bees will love them.

Take time on the weekends to care about YOU!

When we help others, our brain tells us that something good is happening. Helping others is like giving a gift and receiving one back!

GLOSSARY

charity
An organisation that raises money and uses it to help people or animals in need. Charities may also help protect the environment.

donate
To give money or items such as food or clothes to a charity or other good cause. The money or item you donate is called a donation.

community
A group of people who live in the same area. People in a community share schools, hospitals, shops and workplaces. A community can be big or small.

environment
The natural world that surrounds all living things – for example, areas such as beaches and forests. We must try to keep the environment clean and safe for wildlife.

kindness
The ways we show others that we care. Listening, helping with small things and being friendly are all acts of kindness.

mindful
Focusing on your feelings, thoughts and what you can see, hear, smell and touch in the environment around you. Being mindful can help you feel calm.

self-care
Doing things to make sure you feel calm, happy and healthy. When you do kind things for yourself, you are practising self-care.

skill
Something you are good at. For example, drawing, swimming or playing a musical instrument are all skills.

volunteering
Offering your time for free to help with a task – for example, cleaning up litter or helping at a food bank. A person who does volunteering is a volunteer.

worried
Having problems or difficult feelings on your mind. It is normal to worry and have worries. Talk to someone you trust about any worries you have.

INDEX

A
animal rescue centres 25

B
Being Mindful 7

C
charities 25, 26–27
Choose a Chore Stick 11
chores 4, 10–11, 16, 28–29
communities 18, 22–23, 24, 27, 28
Community Kindness Stones 23
community projects 23, 28

D
donations 21, 25, 26–27, 29

F
feelings
    anger 12
    happiness 4–5, 6, 12–13, 16, 18–19, 20, 23, 29
    sadness 4–5, 7, 12, 17, 20, 28
    worry 4, 7, 20
Fill a Donation Box 25
friends 4–5, 8, 12–13, 15, 16, 20–21, 22, 24–25, 28–29

H
How are You? 19

K
kindness 4–5, 8, 15, 19, 21, 23, 28–29
Kindness Calendar 29

L
listening 5, 12

M
Make a Friendship Den 13
Make Happy Jars 5
Make No-Grow Flowers 17
mindfulness 7

N
neighbours 16–17, 22, 24, 26, 28–29

O
Organise a School Bake Sale 27

P
people who help us 15, 18–19
Plan Some Skill Shares 15

S
safety 16–17, 22
saying sorry 12
saying thank you 8, 19
school 20–21, 24, 26–27
self-care 6–7
sharing 8, 10–11, 12, 14–15, 17, 21, 28–29
Smile Experiment 9
smiling 5, 8–9, 16, 18, 23, 28–29
Start a Kindness Club 21

V
volunteering 24–25, 28